AIDA Copywriting for Beginners

By Amanda Symonds

What is AIDA copywriting? 5

How invented AIDA? 6

Why use AIDA? 7

What is conversion copywriting? 8

How can I use the AIDA template to improve my conversions? 10

The Four Elements of AIDA 12

How to use AIDA copywriting 14

Where to Use AIDA in Your Writing 16

What are some examples of AIDA copywriting? 18

AIDA Email Template 23

10 Tips to create engaging ads 28

Why is the AIDA model important? 33

The benefits of AIDA copywriting 34

What is a copywriting formula? 35

Can AI software create copy using AIDA? 39

How does AI copywriting work? 40

So what does this mean for the future of AIDA copywriting? 42

Mistakes to avoid for better conversions 47

12 places to find digital marketing or copywriting jobs 51

Do I need my own website? 56

How to write a compelling pitch for your
copywriting job 58

Conclusion 62

Other books by Amanda Symonds 63

What is AIDA copywriting?

AIDA copywriting is a technique that has been used by marketers and advertisers for many years. It is a way of structuring your message in order to get the most impact and response from your audience. In short, AIDA is a very simple marketing formula that can help you to focus your content so that it's more likely to be successful.

AIDA copywriting is a technique that can be used to create engaging ads, emails, and websites. AIDA stands for Attention, Interest, Desire, and Action. In this book, we will discuss how you can use each of these elements to create an effective marketing message. We'll also provide examples of AIDA copywriting in action so that you can see how it's done correctly. Are you ready to learn more about AIDA copywriting?

How invented AIDA?

The AIDA copywriting technique (or formula) was first developed in the early 1900s by a man named Elias St. Elmo Lewis. He is considered to be the father of modern advertising, and he is credited with creating many of the concepts that are still used in advertising today. AIDA was one of his most famous creations, and it has been used by marketers for over 100 years.

The first step in understanding AIDA copywriting is to know what each letter in the acronym stands for.
Ads are written to catch the readers' attention and hook them in like a fish. (This is Attention)
Once you have their attention, you need to make them interested in what you have to say. You should create a point of interest where readers can continue reading. (This is Interest)
After you have piqued their interest, create a desire for your product or service. You can also state a benefit. (This is Desire)
Finish with a call to action or CTA. (This is Action)

Why use AIDA?

AIDA is an effective marketing tool because it helps you to create a message that will grab attention, interest your audience, and get them to take action. When used correctly, AIDA can be a powerful way to increase sales and conversions.

Most copywriters use this method to increase conversions without even knowing what it is called!

What is conversion copywriting?

Do you want to learn how to write effective calls to action that will help increase your conversion rate? If so, you've come to the right place! In this section, we will discuss what conversion copywriting is and some tips and tricks that will help you write effective CTAs.

Conversion copywriting is the art of writing persuasive, compelling, and actionable text that encourages your readers to take the desired action. This could be anything from signing up for your newsletter to buying your product.

If you want to improve your conversion rate, there are a few things you should keep in mind when crafting your calls to action.

Here are some tips:
- Use strong, active verbs that inspire urgency and excitement (e.g., buy now, sign up today)
- Be clear and concise - get straight to the point
- Make it easy for your reader by including a sense of direction (e.g., click here, fill out this form)

- Use persuasive language that speaks to your reader's needs and desires
- Experiment with different CTAs and see what works best for you and your audience.

Now that we've gone over what conversion copywriting is and some tips to write effective calls to action, let's put it into practice with a quick exercise. Take a look at the following example:

"Our new product is finally here! Order today and get free shipping."

What can be improved about this CTA?

How can I use the AIDA template to improve my conversions?

The AIDA template is a conversion copywriting tool that can be used to improve your conversion rate. To use this template, you will need to craft your CTA in a way that grabs the attention of your reader, interests them in what you have to offer, creates a desire for your product or service, and finally prompts them to take action.

Here's an example of how you could use the AIDA template to improve the CTA we looked at earlier:

"Are you looking for a new product? Our new product is finally here! Order today and get free shipping."

By using the AIDA template, we were able to add a question and improve our CTA by making it more attention-grabbing and persuasive.

Now that you know what conversion copywriting is and how to use the AIDA template, put it into practice and see how it can help improve your conversion rate! Experiment with different CTAs and see what works best for you and your audience. Remember, conversion copywriting is an art, so don't be afraid to get creative!

In this book, we will show you how to use AIDA to create effective marketing messages for your business.

The acronym AIDA stands for Attention, Interest, Desire, and Action.

Copywriters use this technique to grab the attention of their readers, make them interested in what they have to say, create a desire for their product or service, and finally prompt them to take action.

AIDA copywriting can be used in many different marketing materials such as website copy, emails, brochures, and even ads.

If you want to learn more about how to write effective AIDA copy, then keep reading. We will explore all aspects of this technique so that you can start using it in your own marketing materials.

The Four Elements of AIDA

There are four elements that make up the AIDA copywriting process, and they are:

The Hook
The Interest
The Desire
The Action

Each one of these elements is important, and they all work together to create a persuasive message.

The Hook

The hook is the first element of AIDA, and it is used to grab the attention of the reader. The hook should be something that will interest the reader, and it should be something that they will want to read more about.

The Interest

The interest is the second element of AIDA, and it is used to keep the reader interested in what you are saying. The interest should be something that will make the reader want to know more about what you are saying.

The Desire

The desire is the third element of AIDA, and it is used to create a desire in the reader to take action. The desire should be something that will make the reader want to do something, such as buy a product or service.

The Action

The action is the fourth and final element of AIDA, and it is used to persuade the reader to take action. The action should be something that will make the reader want to do something, such as buy a product or service.

How to use AIDA copywriting

There are four steps to using AIDA copywriting in your marketing materials.

Step 1: Get their attention

The first step is to get your readers' attention with an attention-grabbing opening. This could be a powerful statistic, an interesting story, or a question that piques their interest.

Your goal is to make them want to continue reading so that they will reach the next step in the process.

Step 2: Create interest

Now that you have their attention, it's time to make them interested in what you have to say.

You can do this by sharing more information about your product or service and how it can benefit them.

Your goal is to keep them reading so that they will reach the next step in the process.

Step 3: Build desire

The third step is to build desire for your product or service.

You can do this by sharing information about what makes your product or service unique and why they need it in their life.

Your goal is to make them want your product or service so that they will take action.

Step 4: Take action

The final step is to take action with a call-to-action.

Your goal is to prompt your readers to do something such as buy your product, sign up for your newsletter, or visit your website.

AIDA copywriting is a powerful technique that can help you get the most impact and response from your audience. By following these four steps, you can start using it in your own marketing materials today.

Where to Use AIDA in Your Writing

There are many different ways that you can use AIDA in your writing, but here are some of the most common ways:

Sales Letters

AIDA copywriting is often used in sales letters, because it is an effective way to persuade someone to buy a product or service.

Advertising

AIDA copywriting is also used in advertising, because it is an effective way to capture the attention of the reader and to persuade them to take action.

Emails

AIDA copywriting can also be used in emails, because it is a great way to get someone to read your email and to take action.

These are just some of the ways that you can use AIDA copywriting in your own writing but you can use it in lead magnets and other sales material too.

What are some examples of AIDA copywriting?

Some examples of AIDA copywriting for products include:

- A headline that grabbed attention: "Get the perfect summer body with our new weight loss pill!"

- An opening sentence that interests the reader: "Are you tired of being overweight? Our new weight loss pill can help you lose weight quickly and easily!"

- Information that creates a desire for the product: "Our new weight loss pill can help you lose up to 20 pounds in just two weeks!"

- A call to action: "Visit our website today and learn more about our new weight loss pill!"

Looking for a new way to make money? Try [Service] ! We offer [Benefit], and we're always looking for talented individuals to join our team. Click here to learn more and apply today!

Some examples of AIDA copywriting for services include:

If you're looking for a great way to [Benefit], look no further than [Service]!

We offer [Feature], and we're always here to help. Call us today at [Phone Number], or click here to learn more.

Are you ready to take your business to the next level? Then you need [Service]! We offer [Feature], and we're always here to help you succeed. Call us today at [Phone Number], or click here to learn more and get started.

[Service] is the perfect solution for busy people who want to [Benefit]. We offer [Feature], and we're always available to help you get the most out of our service. Click here to learn more, or book in for a free consultation.

Thanks for considering [Service]! We offer [Feature], and we're always here to help you get the most out of our service. Click here to learn more and get started, or call us today at [Phone Number].

If you're looking for a great way to [Benefit], look no further than [Service]! We offer [Feature], and we're always available to help you succeed. Call us today at [Phone Number], or click here to learn more and get started. Thanks for choosing [Service]!

Do you need help with your taxes? Then you need [Service]! We offer tax preparation services for individuals and businesses, and we're always here to help you get the most out of your tax return. Click here to learn more about our services, or call us today at [Phone Number].

Looking for a new job? Then you need [Service]! We offer resume writing and career coaching services, and we're always here to help you find your dream job. Click here to learn more about our services, or call us today at [Phone Number].

Introducing [Service] - the perfect solution for busy people who want to [Benefit]. We offer [Feature], and we're always available to help you get the most out of our service. Click here to learn more and get started, or call us today at [Phone Number].

Thanks for considering [Service]! We offer [Feature], and we're always available to help you get the most out of our service. Click here to learn more, or call us today at [Phone Number]. We look forward to helping you achieve your goals!

Are you ready to take your business to the next level? Then you need [Service]! We offer [Feature], and we're always here to help you succeed. Call us today at [Phone Number], or click here to learn more about our services. Thanks for choosing [Service]!

Do you need help with your taxes? Then you need [Service] ! We offer tax preparation services for individuals and businesses, and we're always here to help you get the most out of your tax return. Click here to learn more about our services, or call us today at [Phone Number].

Looking for a new job? Then you need [Service]! We offer resume writing and career coaching services, and we're always here to help you find your dream job. Click here to learn more about our services, or call us today at [Phone Number]. Thanks for choosing [Service]!

AIDA is a powerful tool that can be used to create effective marketing messages. In this book, we will show you how to use AIDA to create effective marketing messages for your business.

Are you looking for a way to increase your email conversion rates? If so, you need to start using the AIDA email template. This template is designed to help you capture the attention of your readers and persuade them to take action. In this section, we will discuss the AIDA email template and provide an example that you can use for your own business.

AIDA Email Template

The AIDA email template could be loosely divided into four sections: Attention, Interest, Desire, and Action. Each of these sections has a specific purpose and can help you increase your conversion rates. Let's take a closer look at each section.

The Attention section is designed to capture the attention of your readers. You'll want to use headlines and images that are eye-catching and relevant to your message. For example, if you're selling a new product, you might use an image of the product with a headline that says "Introducing the newest addition to our product line."

The Interest section is where you'll pique the interest of your readers. You'll want to provide more information about your product or service here. For example, you might include a video demonstrating how your product works.

The Desire section is where you'll persuade your readers to take action. You'll want to provide compelling reasons why they should buy your product or use your service. For example, you might include customer testimonials or a money-back guarantee.

The Action section is where you'll tell your readers what they need to do next. You'll want to make it easy for them to take action by providing a clear call-to-action button. For example, you might say "Click here to learn more about our new product."

Now that we've discussed the AIDA email template, let's take a look at an example. This example is for a new mascara you are selling.

Subject Line: Introducing the newest addition to our product line

Dear Customer,

Introducing the newest addition to our product line - Bolder mascara! With this new mascara, you'll get longer, fuller lashes that make a statement.

To help you achieve the bold look you desire, we've included a video tutorial on our website. Click here to watch now.

Image of customer testimonial or review for social proof.

Bolder mascara is available now, so click here to order yours today. We know you're going to love it! If you don't, we have a money back guarantee.

Sincerely,

Your Name

Brand name

What else you need to remember?

Try the following:

- A good subject line is essential for grabbing attention and getting a decent open rate. Make sure your subject is clear, concise, and engaging. Emoticons may help depending on your audience.

- A strong opening sentence can also be very effective at getting attention. Use an interesting statistic or fact to start your email off on the right foot.

- Some explanation about your brand and product or service is needed here to help your audience feel their problem or need could be helped by you. They need to become consciously aware that they could benefit from your service.

- Keep your message relevant to your audience. They will lose interest if you start talking about topics that don't concern them.

- Use strong language to create desire. Words like "amazing," "unbelievable," and "incredible" can help increase the desire for your product or service.

 Content above the CTA can be used to increase conversions, such as:
-Before and after photos
-Videos explaining benefits
-Social Proof or testimonies

FOMO (fear of missing out) is also a useful tool to get people to take action. By creating a sense of urgency and making people feel like they need to act now, you can encourage them to take the desired action. Discount codes, course closure dates, access to free giveaways and other special bonuses or privileges help create this feeling.

10 Tips to create engaging ads

Now that you know the basics of AIDA copywriting, here are a few tips to help you create even more engaging ads:

1. AIDA copywriting is not just for ads! You can also use this technique when writing emails and website content.

2. A good headline is essential for grabbing attention. Make sure your headline is clear, concise, and interesting.

3. A strong opening sentence can also be very effective at getting attention. Use an interesting statistic or fact to start your ad off on the right foot.

4. Keep your message relevant to your audience. They will lose interest if you start talking about topics that don't concern them.

5. Use strong language to create desire. Words like "amazing," "unbelievable," and "incredible" can help increase the desire for your product or service.

6. Use images and videos sparingly. Too many visuals can be overwhelming and will actually decrease interest.

7. Make sure your call to action is clear and concise. Tell them exactly what you want them to do, such as "call now" or "click here."

8. AIDA copywriting is not a one-size-fits-all solution. Be creative and experiment with different techniques until you find what works best for you.

10. Always test your ads before you publish them. A/B testing is a great way to see which version of your ad is more effective.

AIDA copywriting is a powerful tool that can help you create engaging marketing messages. By using the AIDA technique, you can make sure that your message will stand out and get noticed by potential customers. So don't wait any longer, start using AIDA copywriting today!

Here are a few things to keep in mind when using AIDA copywriting:

- Use a headline or opening sentence that will grab attention.
- Keep the message relevant to your audience.
- Use strong language to create desire.
- Make sure your call to action is clear.
- A/B test your ads before you publish them.

Nike, Coca-Cola, and Apple have all utilized AIDA marketing. There is an art to this that they master when it comes to defining their consumer base and aiming directly at their intended audience. The companies have strong, attention-grabbing commercial advertisements in all media (print, television, social media, etc.).

For example, the Nike ad with Colin Kaepernick received a lot of attention when it first came out. The ad was designed to create interest and desire in the product by using a controversial figure. It also prompted action by including a call-to-action at the end of the ad. This example shows how AIDA copywriting can be used to create an effective advertisement.

AIDA Ad Example:

Opening Sentence:

Looking to create more engaging ads? AIDA copywriting may be just what you need!

This opening sentence grabs attention by promising to provide a solution to a common problem. It then creates interest by providing relevant information about AIDA copywriting. Finally, it creates desire by mentioning how this technique can help improve ad performance.

Example headline: AIDA Copywriting: How to Write Engaging Ads, Emails, and Websites
This headline is compelling because it tells the reader what they can expect to learn from the article. It also uses keywords that are relevant to the topic of AIDA copywriting. By including these keywords, potential readers can find this article more easily when searching online.

Example call to action:

Ready to start using AIDA copywriting in your own ads? Check out our latest ebook for everything you need to know!

This call to action is clear and concise, telling the reader precisely what they need to do next. By including a link to our ebook, we make it easy for readers to access more information on this topic.

Why is the AIDA model important?

Because it helps you create content that is focused and relevant to your audience. If you are asked to audit advertising that isn't working, more often than not you'll find that it doesn't adhere to AIDA. The advertising may fail to gain interest, or perhaps it doesn't create desire. It may be too difficult to convert and take action on.

AIDA copywriting can help to identify these problems and by explaining the formula to the brand and business owners, then reworking the advertising campaign you can move forward to create a successful campaign for you and your client!

The benefits of AIDA copywriting

There are many benefits to using AIDA copywriting in your marketing materials.

Some of the benefits include:
· Getting more attention from your readers
· Creating interest in what you have to say
· Building desire for your product or service
· Prompting your readers to take action

If you want to get the most impact and response from your audience, then using AIDA copywriting is a great way to do it.

What is a copywriting formula?

A copywriting formula is a set of guidelines that you can use to create effective marketing messages. The AIDA formula is one of the most popular and widely used formulas. AIDA is a great copywriting technique, but it's not the only one out there and it certainly isn't the be-all, end-all of writing great copy.

I've used it successfully in the past, but there have been times when it just didn't work for the piece I was writing.

That's why I wanted to write this section and share some other great copywriting techniques that you can use instead of, or in addition to, AIDA.

1. PAS: Problem, Agitate, Solution

2. The Rule of Three

3. The before-during-after

4. The Anecdote

5. The Testimonial

No matter what copywriting technique you use, remember that the goal is always to write something that will stop the reader in their tracks, make them think, and then take action. If you can do that, you're well on your way to writing great copy!

Here are five other great techniques you can use to write compelling copy.

1. PAS: Problem, Agitate, Solution

The PAS technique is all about painting a picture of the problem your reader is facing, agitating that problem so they really feel it, and then offering a solution.

2. The Rule of Three

The rule of three is a literary principle that suggests things that come in threes are inherently more pleasing, effective, and memorable than other numbers of things.

3. The before-during-after

The before-during-after technique is exactly what it sounds like—it's a way of telling your reader's story by showing what their life was like before they used your product or service, what it was like during, and what it's like now.

4. The Anecdote

An anecdote is a short, usually personal story that's used to illustrate a point.

5. The Testimonial

A testimonial is a quote from a satisfied customer that vouches for your product or service.

Can AI software create copy using AIDA?

Yes, there are AI software programs that can create AIDA sales copy for you. However, it's important to remember that AIDA copywriting is more than just a formula – it's an art. So, while AI software can create AIDA ads, they may not be as effective as ads created by a human copywriter who understands the nuances of AIDA copywriting. So using them for inspiration and getting a first draft done using an AI tool can be a great way to remove writer's block and get your creative juices flowing.

How does AI copywriting work?

AI copywriting works by using algorithms to generate text that adheres to the AIDA formula. The software looks at a set of data points and then writes copy that is designed to grab attention, create interest, desire, and prompt action. It uses sentiment analysis, readability scores and emotional tone and other techniques to understand what kind of message will be most effective.

It can write content for any source: social media, Google or Bing ads, website copy for product or landing pages, articles or blog posts.

It also uses persuasive terms in the copy to grab attention and interest, connect to your audience and prompt action. It also knows which target keywords Google wants you to use to rank higher in SERPs (search engine results pages).

Machines are getting better and better at understanding human language, and they're only going to get better. This means that copywriters will have to be more and more creative in order to

stand out. They'll need to come up with new ways
to grab attention and write compelling copy.

So what does this mean for the future of AIDA copywriting?

AI will make it easier to collect data about customer behaviour and preferences. This data can then be used to write more targeted and effective copy. Copywriters will need to be able to understand and analyze this data in order to use it effectively.

Machines will also be able to write copy themselves. This doesn't mean that copywriters will be out of a job, however. Machines can't yet match humans when it comes to creativity and understanding context. Copywriters will still be needed to come up with new ideas and to write copy that is truly compelling.

Introducing Jasper AI

Jasper AI software was first developed several years ago to help businesses automate the writing of marketing and sales copy. It is one of the oldest.

It has read 50% of the internet and can put together engaging and compelling content for you in minutes, rather than hours. It can write new copy and also rewrite old campaigns for you to improve conversion and keep everything on brand. I use it to keep picky clients happy and can rewrite content in any tone of voice and even mimic their brand by pasting their website copy into the software and hitting compose!

In 2022, Jasper has been continuously expanded and updated with new features, including AI Art, making it the best AI software for marketing or sales copy today! Visit https://jasper.ai/?fpr=greenbubz to get a free trial with 10,000 words.

Jasper comes with a wide range of templates that you can use to write your marketing or sales copy. You can write content for ads, emails, blog posts, lead magnets and landing pages. These 50+ templates are designed by marketing experts and have been tested and proven to be effective. You can also customize the templates to fit your specific needs and create Recipes to write books (just like this one).

How does Jasper AI create AIDA copy?

Jasper AI creates AIDA copy by first understanding your audience and what you want to achieve with your ad. It then uses natural language processing to create an attention-grabbing headline and body copy that will interest your target audience and prompt them to take action.

You outline the product description and a tone of voice and Jasper writes the rest. You can delete and keep reworking your commands to get the copy written that you like.

Features

Some of the key features that make Jasper the best AI software for writing marketing or sales copy include:

- Its ability to understand the context of a situation and provide relevant information.

- Its ability to generate catchy headlines and copy that packs a punch.

- Its ability to help you come up with clever phrases and condense research in minutes (fact checking is still required as the online information that Jasper analyses is often incorrect).

Here are some AIDA examples written by Jasper AI.

Example 1: Great Wrap

Attention: Eco-friendly plastic wrap that is safe for your food and the environment

Interest: Plastic wrap is a necessary evil in the kitchen, but it doesn't have to be. Great Wrap is made of plant based materials so it's biodegradable and compostable. It also has a higher heat tolerance than traditional plastic wrap, so you can use it for all your cooking needs.

Desire: Not only is Great Wrap better for the environment, but it also works better than traditional plastic wrap. You can use it to cover bowls, pack sandwiches, or store leftovers. Plus, the adhesive strip seals tightly so your food stays fresh.

Action: Try Great Wrap today! It's available on our website.

If you're looking for help with AIDA copywriting, or any other kind of copywriting, try a Jasper AI trial today. You can receive 10,000 free credits to use on their AI-powered copywriting platform. With Jasper, you can create AIDA copy that's tailored to your specific audience and designed to achieve your desired results. So why not give it a try? You could be surprised at just how effective AIDA copy can be.

Jasper offers a free trial with 10000 credits to use on the AIDA copywriting platform. You can create AIDA copy that is tailored to your specific brand, audience and designed to achieve your desired results. So why not give it a try?

Visit: https://jasper.ai/?fpr=greenbubz today.

Mistakes to avoid for better conversions

If you're looking to improve your website's conversion rate, you need to make sure that you're not making any of the following AIDA mistakes. These mistakes can be costly and can hurt your business's bottom line.

The first AIDA mistake is failing to identify your target audience. If you don't know who your target audience is, you won't be able to effectively market to them. Take the time to research your target audience and create buyer personas. This will help you better understand their needs and how to appeal to them.

Another common AIDA mistake is not having a clear call-to-action (CTA). Your CTA should be easy to spot and should tell visitors what you want them to do next. Make sure that your CTA is relevant to the content on your page and that it's easy for visitors to find.

Yet another common mistake is not providing enough information about your product or service. If visitors can't quickly and easily understand what you're offering, they're likely to move on to another website. Make sure that your website copy is clear and concise. Use easy-to-understand language and include pricing information up front.

The fourth AIDA mistake is failing to create a sense of urgency. If visitors don't feel a sense of urgency, they're less likely to take action. Use strong language and persuasive techniques to encourage visitors to act now.

Finally, the fifth AIDA mistake is not following up with leads. Just because someone fills out a form on your website doesn't mean they're ready to buy. You need to follow up with leads through email or phone calls in order to close the sale.

Avoiding these five AIDA mistakes will help you improve your website's conversion rate and grow your marketing or copywriting business.Become an expert copywriter

Copywriting is the art of writing persuasive, interesting, and compelling copy that will convince people to take action. It's not just about writing well;

it's about understanding your audience and knowing how to craft an effective message that will get them to take the desired action.

Joining a supportive online community can help you move forward and avoid making painful mistakes at the start by learning from others, you may also find a good mentor in the process. Reading as many books and blog posts on the subject, watching AIDA copywriting tutorials and completing an online course. By taking the time to prepare yourself with quality resources, you'll be well on your way to mastering this important skill.

Once you understand the basics of copywriting, you need to start practicing. The best way to do this is by taking on some small projects for friends or family members. Offer to write a sales letter for their business, or create an email campaign for their next product launch. Not only will this give you some real-world experience, but it will also help you build your portfolio and show potential clients what you're capable of.

As you start to get more experience, you can begin to take on larger projects. There are plenty of opportunities for freelance copywriters, so don't be afraid to put yourself out there and start pitching your services. You may even want to consider starting your own copywriting business; with the right marketing and a few good clients, you could be well on your way to success.

In just one month, with dedication and hard work, you can become a copywriting expert. By following the steps in this chapter, you'll be well on your way to crafting compelling copy that will help you achieve your business goals.

12 places to find digital marketing or copywriting jobs

If you're a freelance writer, finding copywriting jobs can be a daunting task. With so many different sites and sources, it can be hard to know where to start. In this chapter, we will discuss 12 of the best places to find copywriting jobs online. We'll provide tips on how to find the best gigs for your skills and experience, as well as advice on how to get started in this competitive industry!

So, where can you find copywriting jobs? Here are twelve of the best places to start your search:

- Indeed.com: Indeed is a great resource for finding all sorts of jobs, including copywriting positions. Simply type "copywriter" into the search bar and filter by location and job type (full-time, contract, etc.) to find openings in your area.

- Craigslist: Believe it or not, Craigslist can be a great place to find freelance writing gigs. Just head to your local Craigslist page and search for "copywriter" under the "Jobs" section. You may have to wade through a few non-writing related positions, but there are often quality copywriting jobs posted here!

- LinkedIn: LinkedIn is a great place to find both full-time and freelance writing gigs. Start by searching for "copywriter" in the Jobs section, or try looking for relevant groups that you can join. Once you're a member of these groups, you'll have access to job postings as well as networking opportunities with other professionals in the field.

- FreelanceWritingGigs.com: As the name suggests, this site is dedicated to helping freelance writers find writing gigs. Simply browse through the available jobs or search for positions that match your skills and experience. You can also sign up for their newsletter to get new job listings delivered straight to your inbox!

- Contently: Contently is a great resource for both copywriters and businesses looking to hire them. The site allows you to create a profile and portfolio, making it easy to showcase your work to potential clients. You can also search for jobs or browse through available projects.

- Upwork: Upwork is one of the most popular freelance job sites out there, and for good reason. It's easy to use and provides access to a wide range of clients and projects. Simply create a profile, find relevant jobs, and apply!

- Fiverr: Fiverr is a great option for copywriters just starting out as it offers gigs starting at just $ five! You can create a gig listing that outlines your services and what you're willing to do for that price. Once you find a buyer, simply complete the project and get paid!

- PeoplePerHour: PeoplePerHour is another great option for finding freelance writing jobs. Simply create a profile and browse through the available gigs. When you find a gig that interests you, simply send a proposal outlining your qualifications and experience.

- Guru: Guru is similar to other freelance job sites in that it allows you to find jobs and submit proposals. However, one unique feature of this site is that it also allows businesses to post "contests" for copywriters. This can be a great way to get your foot in the door with new clients!

- Glassdoor: Glassdoor is a great resource for finding full-time jobs, but did you know that it can also be used to find freelance writing gigs? Just type "copywriter" into the search bar and filter by location and job type (full-time, contract, etc.) to find openings in your area.

- Jasper.ai's Facebook group has a weekly job board where you can advertise that your skills are for hire (using Jasper.ai of course).

- The Creative Group: The Creative Group is a staffing agency that specializes in finding jobs for creatives, including freelance writers. Simply create a profile and upload your resume so that potential clients can find you. You can also search through their job listings and apply directly to the ones that interest you.

With these sites, you should have no trouble finding quality copywriting gigs! Just remember to put your best foot forward and be professional at all times –

this will help you stand out from the competition and land the job! Good luck!

Do I need my own website?

There's no doubt about it — having your own website is a huge advantage when you're a copywriter. It gives you a place to showcase your work, connect with potential clients, and even sell your services. But there are also some drawbacks to consider before making the decision to create or not create a website. In this chapter, we'll take a look at the pros and cons of having your own website as a copywriter.

On the plus side, having your own website gives you a great platform to showcase your skills and services. You can create portfolio pages, post samples of some of your best work, and provide clients with detailed descriptions of how you can help them accomplish their goals.

Furthermore, having a website makes it easier for prospective customers to get in touch with you and learn more about the services you offer. You can detail which packages you have available and charge more for your services.

However, there are also some negatives associated with having an Aida copywriter's website. One is that it takes time and energy to design and maintain a website. You'll need to be familiar with Wordpress, as well as have good graphic design skills if you want your site to look professional. Additionally, creating and maintaining a website can be expensive, as you'll likely need to pay for web hosting and other services.

And finally, it's important to remember that having a website won't guarantee more clients or better sales — you still need to actively promote your site in order for it to be successful.

So, you are better off working on any of the 12 platforms I mentioned above until you get some regular clients.

Ultimately, it's up to you to decide which option works best for you and your business.

How to write a compelling pitch for your copywriting job

1. Define your audience.

Before you can start writing your pitch, you need to know who your audience is. Who are you trying to reach with your pitch? What are their needs and wants? What are their pain points? Once you have a good understanding of your audience, you can start crafting a pitch that will resonate with them.\

2. Research the company.

Before you start writing, take some time to research the company you're pitching to. Find out as much as you can about their business, their target market, and their specific needs. This will help you to write a more targeted and effective pitch.

3. Write a compelling headline.

Your headline is the first thing that your audience will see, so it needs to be attention-grabbing and relevant. It should give the reader an idea of what your pitch is about and make them want to read more.

4. Keep it short and sweet.

Your pitch should be concise and to the point. No one wants to read a long, rambling email, so make sure that you get straight to the point. The shorter your pitch is, the more likely it is that your audience will read it all the way through.

5. Highlight your experience.

Be sure to highlight any relevant experience that you have in your pitch. If you have copywriting experience, be sure to mention it! Your audience will want to know that you have the skills and experience necessary to do the job well.

6. Showcase your samples.

If you have any relevant samples of your work, be sure to include them in your pitch! This will give your audience a good idea of what kind of work you are capable of and whether or not you would be a good fit for their needs.

7. Explain what makes you unique.

What makes you different from all of the other copywriters out there? Why should your audience choose you over someone else? Be sure to highlight what makes you unique in your pitch so that your audience knows what they would be getting if they chose to work with you.

8. Offer a solution to their problem.

Your audience has a problem that they need solved, and they need a copywriter to help them do it! In your pitch, explain how you can help them solve their problem and why you are the best person for the job.

9. Provide a call to action.

Your pitch should always include a call to action so that your audience knows what they need to do next. Do you want them to email you back? Give you a call? Set up a meeting? Whatever it is, be sure to include it in your pitch!

10. Proofread before sending!

This one seems like a no-brainer, but it's important enough that it bears repeating: Always proofread your pitches before sending them out! Nothing will turn off an potential client faster than receiving a pitch full of typos and grammatical errors, so take the time to proofread before hitting "send".

Conclusion

We hope this book has helped you learn the techniques of AIDA Copywriting and become a better copywriter and digital marketer. Please remember to leave a review to help others find this book and encourage us to keep writing.

Other books by Amanda Symonds

Open Water Diver

Rescue Diver

Power Phrases for Performance Reviews

End Writer's Block

Secret AI Ghostwriter

300 Online Dating Profile Phrases

Create Your Own Escape Room